© 1999 Havoc Publishing
Artwork © 1999 Teresa Kogut

ISBN 1-57977-159-9

Published by Havoc Publishing
San Diego, California

Made in China

Please write to us for more information
on Havoc Publishing products.

www.havocpub.com

Havoc Publishing
9808 Waples Street
San Diego, California 92121
U.S.A.

This Book Celebrates the Friendship of:

Francesco Vecchio

and

Clara Vera Nicola

Contents

Friends Forever
Growing Together
How We Met
How We Are Alike
Things We Don't Like
Sharing Our Differences
Families Are Near To The Heart
Photographs
Lending a Helping Hand
You Stood by Me
Some Similarities
Saying Funny Things
Treasured Times
Photographs
Days Spent Together

Contents

Going Out on the Town
A Birthday Wish
Travel Memories
Special Occasions
Celebrating Holidays
Photographs
A Story to Pass On
Memories of Our Friendship
Things We Admire Each Other
Times We Missed Each Other
From Our Kitchens
Notes of Friendship
Our Future Wishes
Photographs
Five Years From Now

Beary Best Friends

©T.Kogut98

We are friends forever
sharing our lives together

Our friendship is beary special because _____

_____

_____

_____

_____

_____

_____

_____

As we have grown,
true friendship we have known

My name _____ Your name _____

My birth date _____ Your birth date _____

Where I grew up _____ Where you grew up _____

We share these interests and hobbies _____

_____

_____

_____

My education _____ Your education _____

Things I enjoy _____

Things you enjoy _____

Important people in my life _____

_____

Important people in your life _____

_____

When I met you I quickly knew
that we would be friends thru and thru

This is the story about where we met _____

_____

We remember that _____ introduced us to each other.

I remember my first impression of you was _____

_____

_____

_____

What was your first impression of me? _____

_____

_____

Bee Free

Home Sweet Home

Do you remember this story about the day we met? _____

_____

_____

_____

_____

_____

_____

_____

_____

_____

Bee Free

Home Sweet Home

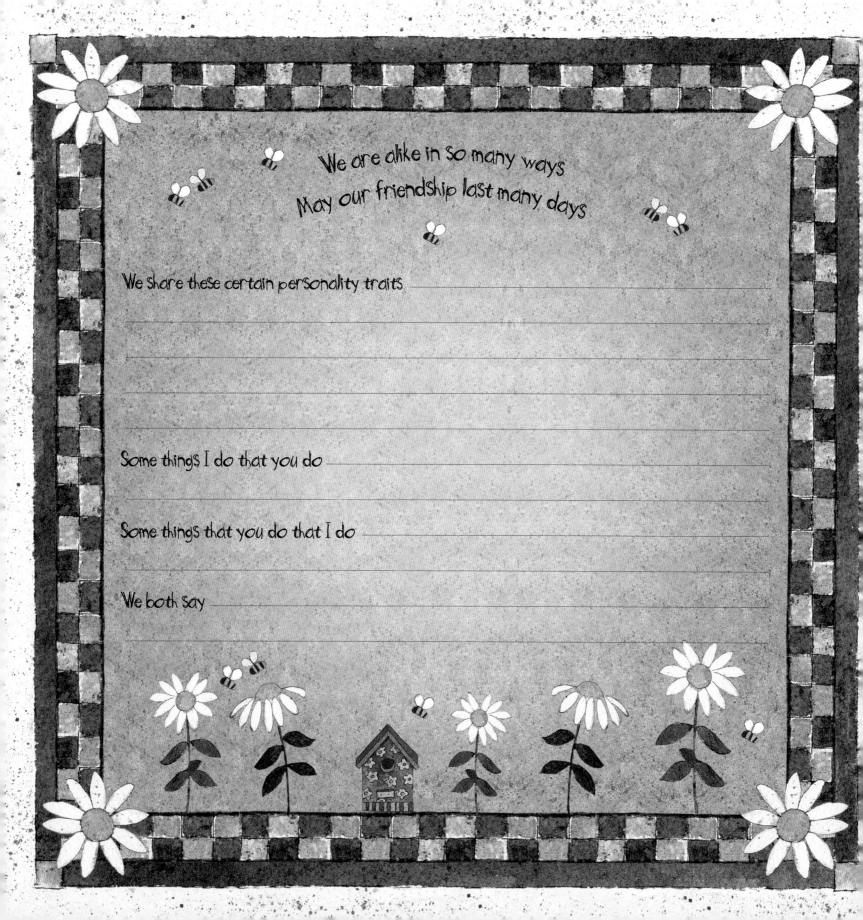

We are alike in so many ways
May our friendship last many days

We share these certain personality traits _____

_____

_____

_____

Some things I do that you do _____

_____

Some things that you do that I do _____

_____

We both say _____

_____

We have the best time and find the best sales at these stores _____

_____

The best movies that we have seen together are _____

_____

We remember sharing these books and talking about these authors _____

_____

Our favorite shows on television are _____

_____

Some of our favorite songs and music are _____

_____

Our favorite restaurant that we like to go to together is _____

_____

Our favorite dessert to order is _____

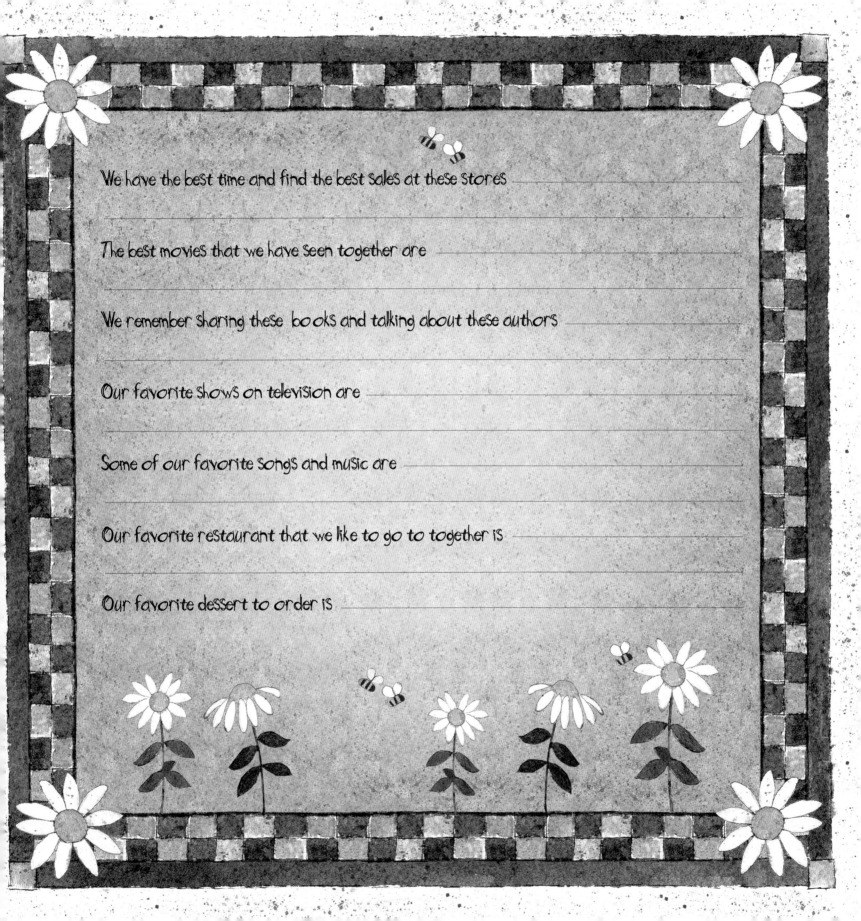

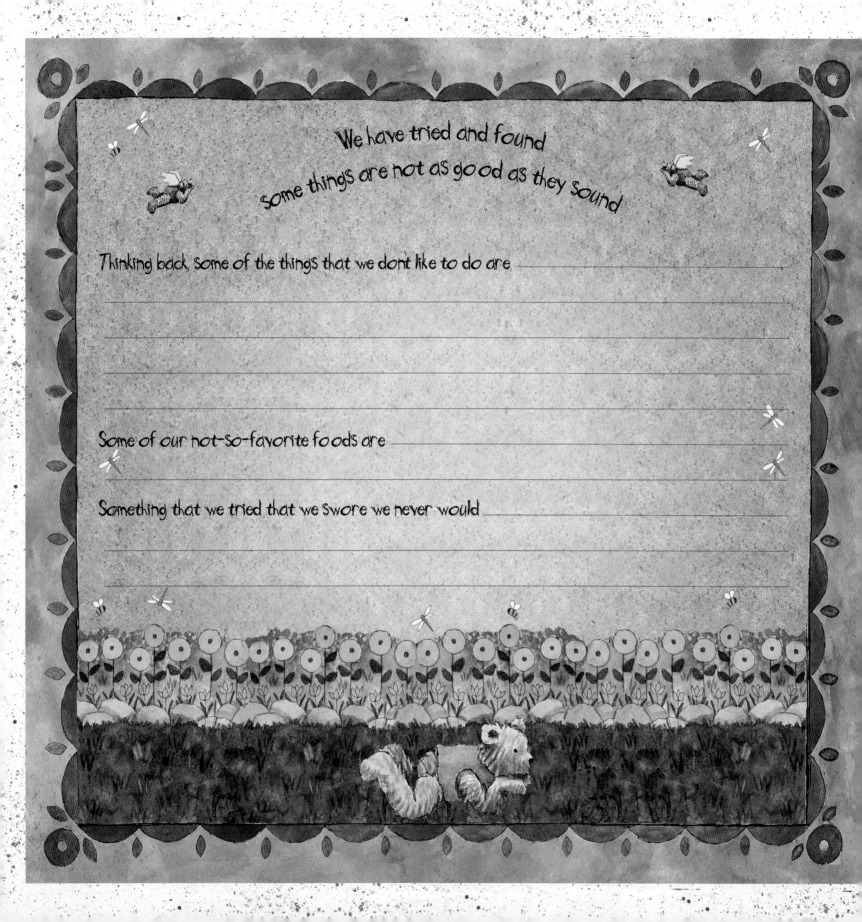

We have tried and found
Some things are not as good as they sound

Thinking back, some of the things that we don't like to do are _____

_____

_____

_____

_____

Some of our not-so-favorite foods are _____

_____

Something that we tried that we swore we never would _____

_____

_____

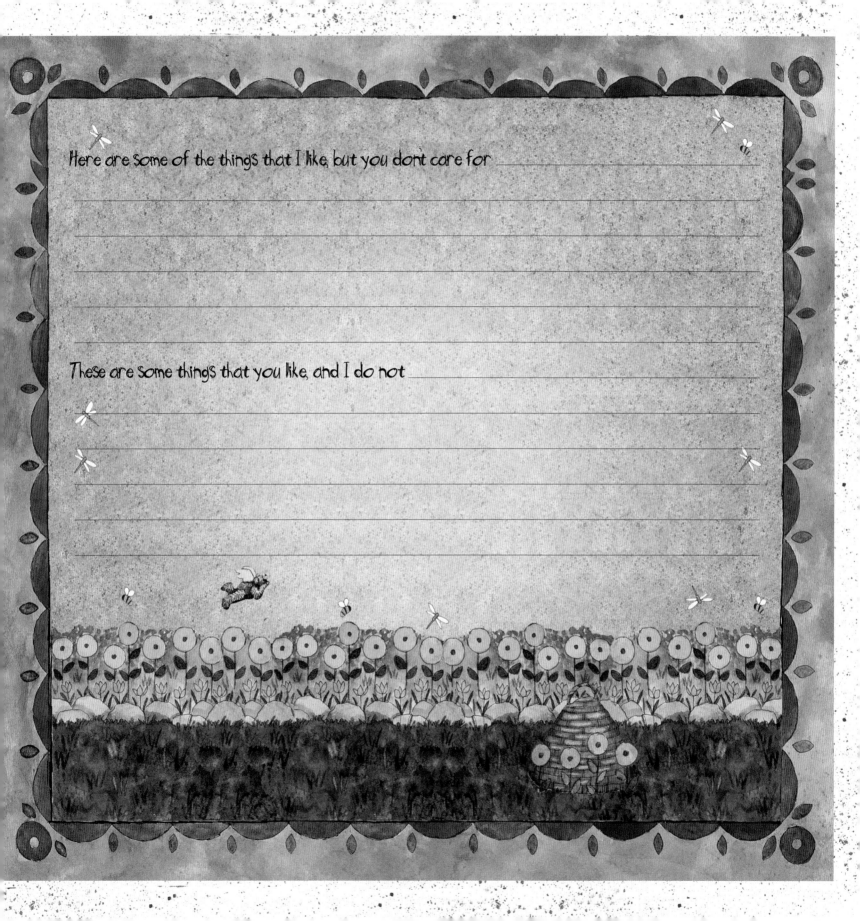

Here are some of the things that I like, but you don't care for _____

_____

_____

_____

_____

These are some things that you like, and I do not _____

_____

_____

_____

_____

©T.Kogut 98

We are different I am aware
but our unique qualities allow us more to share

Our personalities are different in these ways _____

_____

_____

This is how we are different emotionally _____

_____

We feel that our differences make our friendship stronger because _____

_____

_____

_____

Families are near to the heart
In our lives they play an important part.

It is fun to remember these stories about times spent with both our families _____

_____

_____

_____

_____

_____

We have fond memories of these holidays spent together _____

_____

_____

_____

_____

_____

photograph

photograph

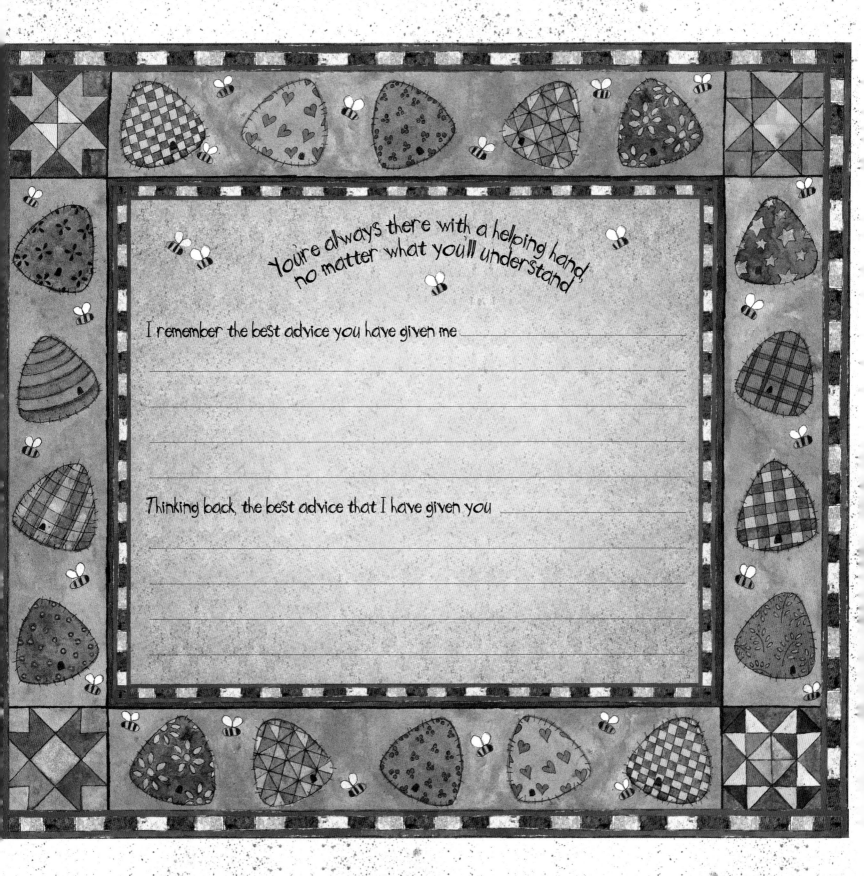

You're always there with a helping hand,
no matter what you'll understand

I remember the best advice you have given me _____

_____

_____

_____

Thinking back, the best advice that I have given you _____

_____

_____

_____

A friend stands by you
And helps to guide you

I recall that I needed you the most when _____

_____

_____

and you needed me when _____

_____

_____

I remember I helped you when _____

_____

_____

and you helped me out when _____

_____

I remember this time when you understood me when no one else did _____

_____

_____

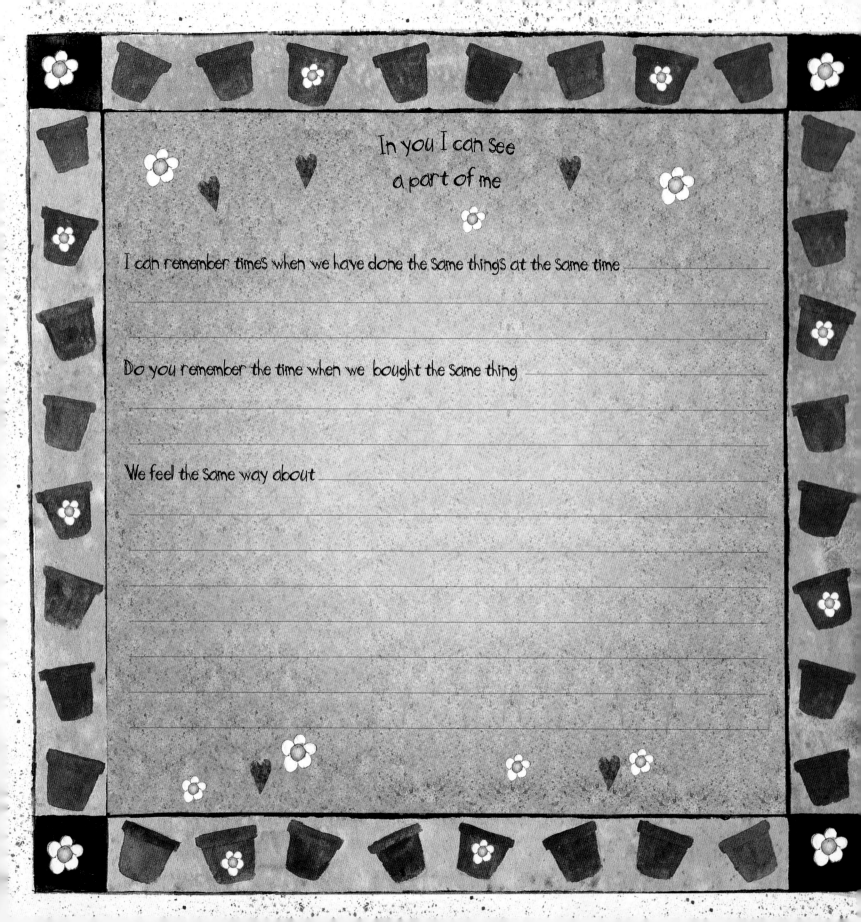

In you I can see
a part of me

I can remember times when we have done the same things at the same time

_____

_____

Do you remember the time when we bought the same thing _____

_____

_____

We feel the same way about _____

_____

_____

_____

_____

_____

_____

You brighten my day
with the sweet things you say

I remember these funny things you've said _____

_____

_____

Funny things that I have said _____

_____

_____

We have our own special ways of saying _____

_____

_____

Some of the nicknames that we have for each other are _____

_____

I've begun to say this just like you _____

_____

_____

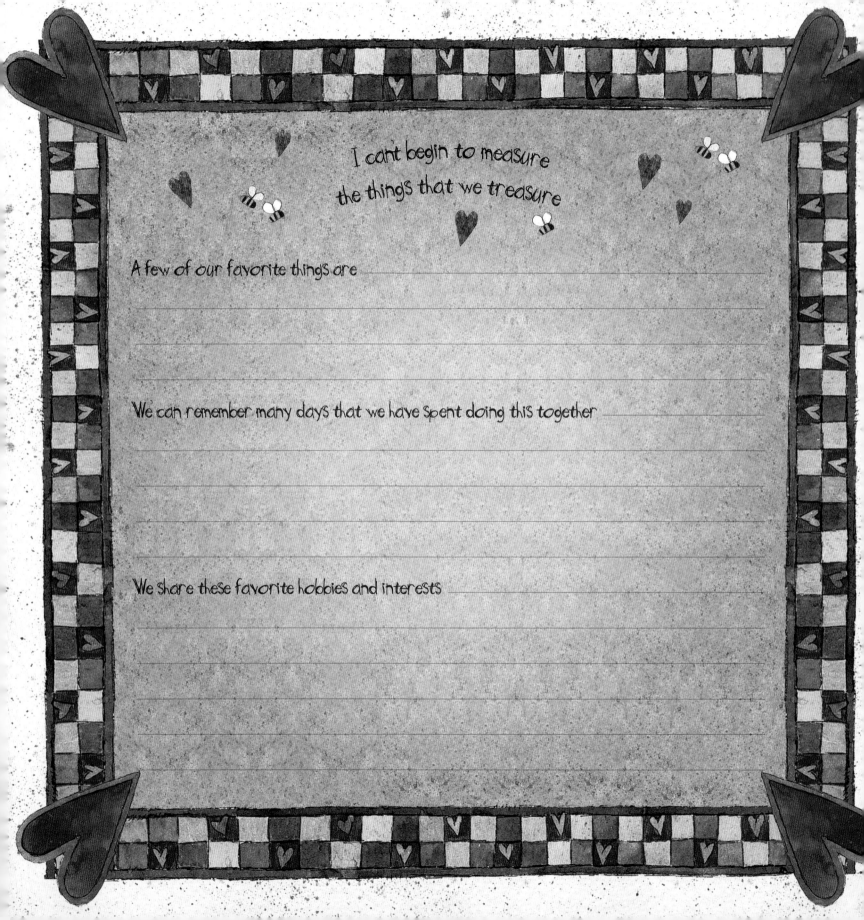

I can't begin to measure
the things that we treasure

A few of our favorite things are _____

_____

_____

_____

We can remember many days that we have spent doing this together _____

_____

_____

_____

_____

We share these favorite hobbies and interests _____

_____

_____

_____

_____

_____

FRIENDS to the END

photograph

photograph

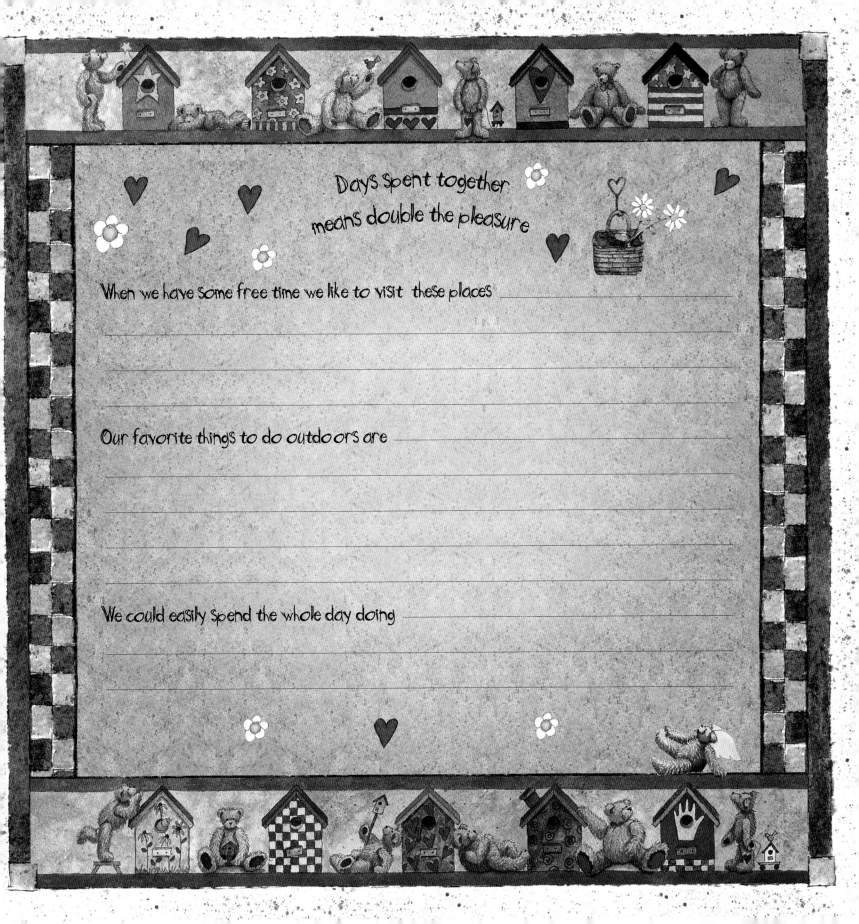

Days spent together
means double the pleasure

When we have some free time we like to visit these places _____

_____

_____

Our favorite things to do outdoors are _____

_____

_____

_____

We could easily spend the whole day doing _____

_____

_____

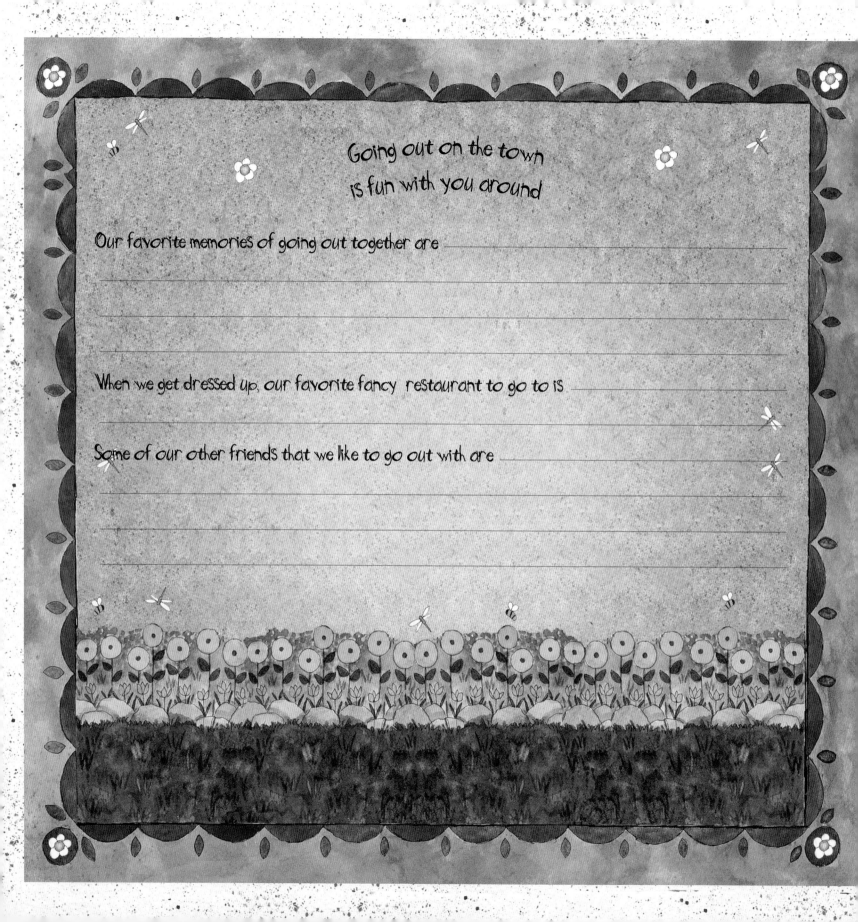

Going out on the town
is fun with you around

Our favorite memories of going out together are _____

_____

_____

_____

When we get dressed up, our favorite fancy restaurant to go to is _____

_____

Some of our other friends that we like to go out with are _____

_____

_____

_____

Our wildest and craziest story is about the time we _____

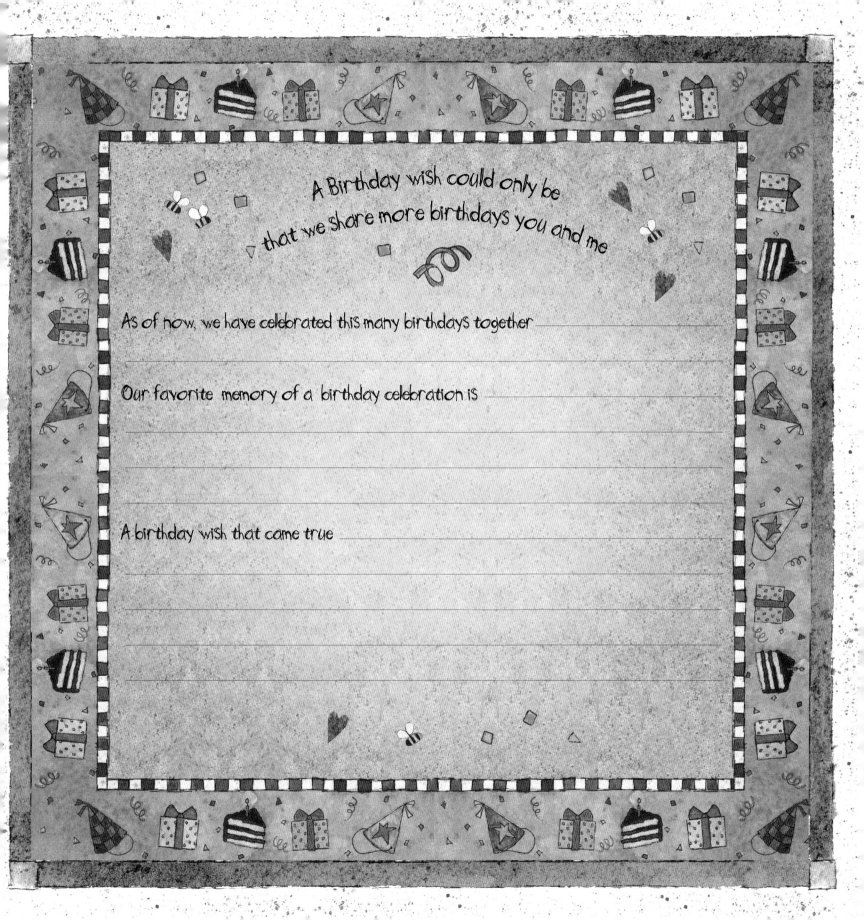

A Birthday wish could only be
that we share more birthdays you and me

As of now, we have celebrated this many birthdays together

Our favorite memory of a birthday celebration is

A birthday wish that came true

The times I treasure
are when we've traveled together

Our fondest memories of vacations that we have taken together are _____

_____

_____

Our favorite vacation story is about the time we _____

_____

_____

_____

If we could get away today, we would be off to _____

_____

_____

_____

Attach favorite tickets, receipts and other mementos here

Whether with joy or tears
I'm glad we've shared these years

These are some special occasions that we have celebrated together _____

_____

_____

A milestone that we have reached together _____

_____

_____

_____

These are some goals that we have set together and met _____

_____

_____

_____

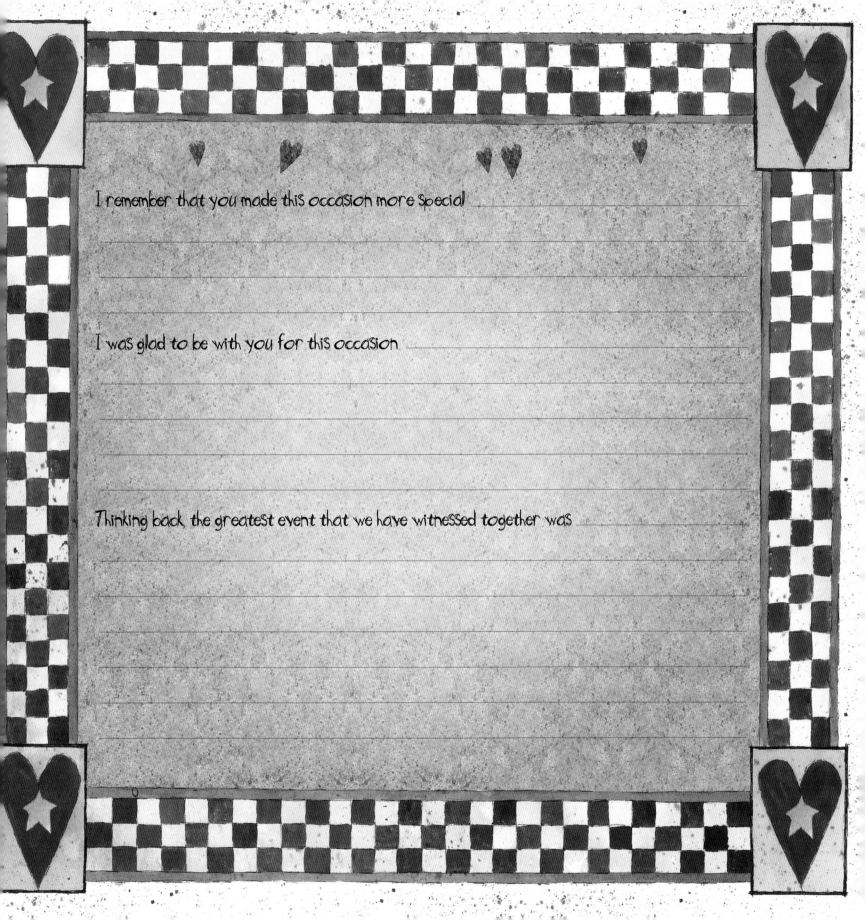

I remember that you made this occasion more special

I was glad to be with you for this occasion

Thinking back, the greatest event that we have witnessed together was

During the holidays we share our cheer
and celebrate with fun throughout the year

Our favorite holiday to celebrate together is _____

_____

_____

_____

We remember these special gifts we have exchanged over the years _____

_____

_____

_____

A special holiday tradition that we share together is _____

_____

_____

_____

_____

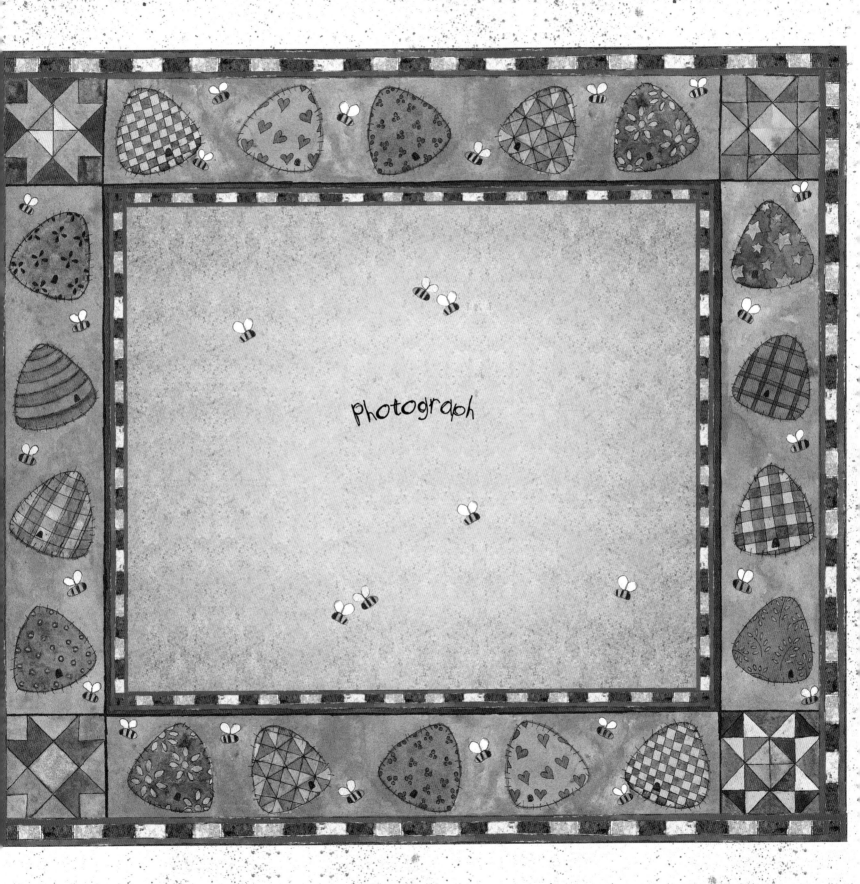

photograph

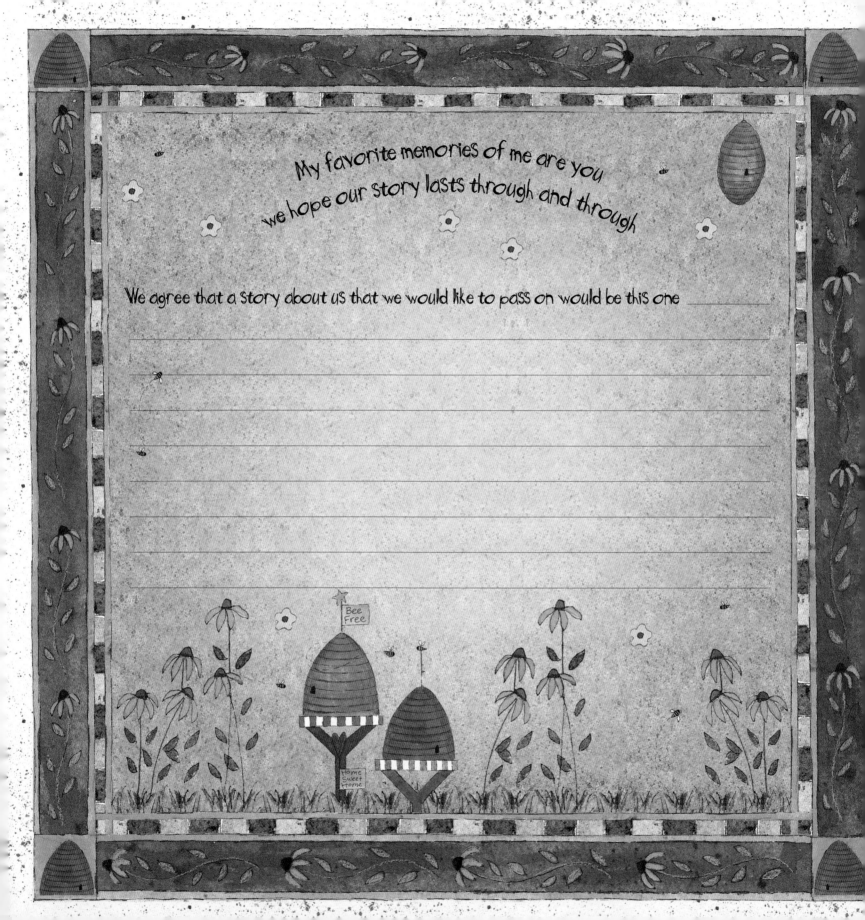

My favorite memories of me are you
we hope our story lasts through and through

We agree that a story about us that we would like to pass on would be this one _____

_____

_____

_____

_____

_____

_____

Bee Free

Home Sweet Home

Our Favorite Memories

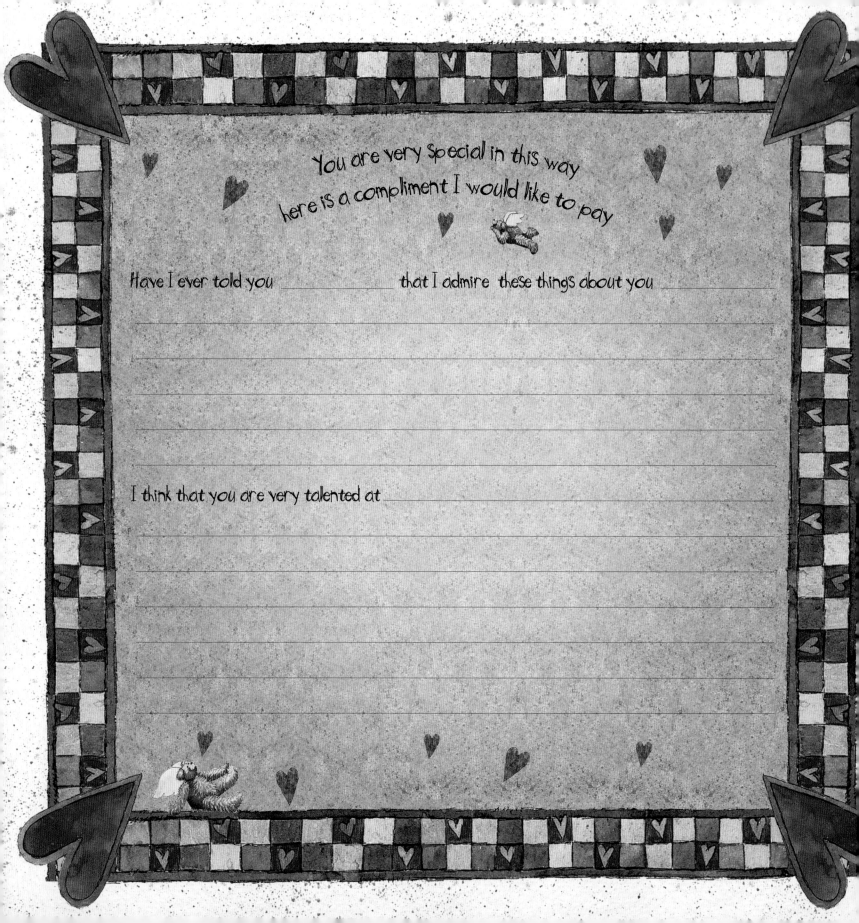

You are very special in this way
here is a compliment I would like to pay

Have I ever told you _____ that I admire these things about you _____

_____

_____

_____

I think that you are very talented at _____

_____

_____

_____

_____

And here is a compliment I will pay you
I admire these things about you too

Have I ever told you _____ that I admire these things about you _____

_____

_____

_____

_____

I think that you are very talented at _____

_____

_____

_____

_____

_____

There was a time when I missed you lots
but you were always in my heart and thoughts

We remember that we missed each other the most when _____

_____

_____

_____

We wish we could have been together when _____

_____

_____

_____

_____

_____

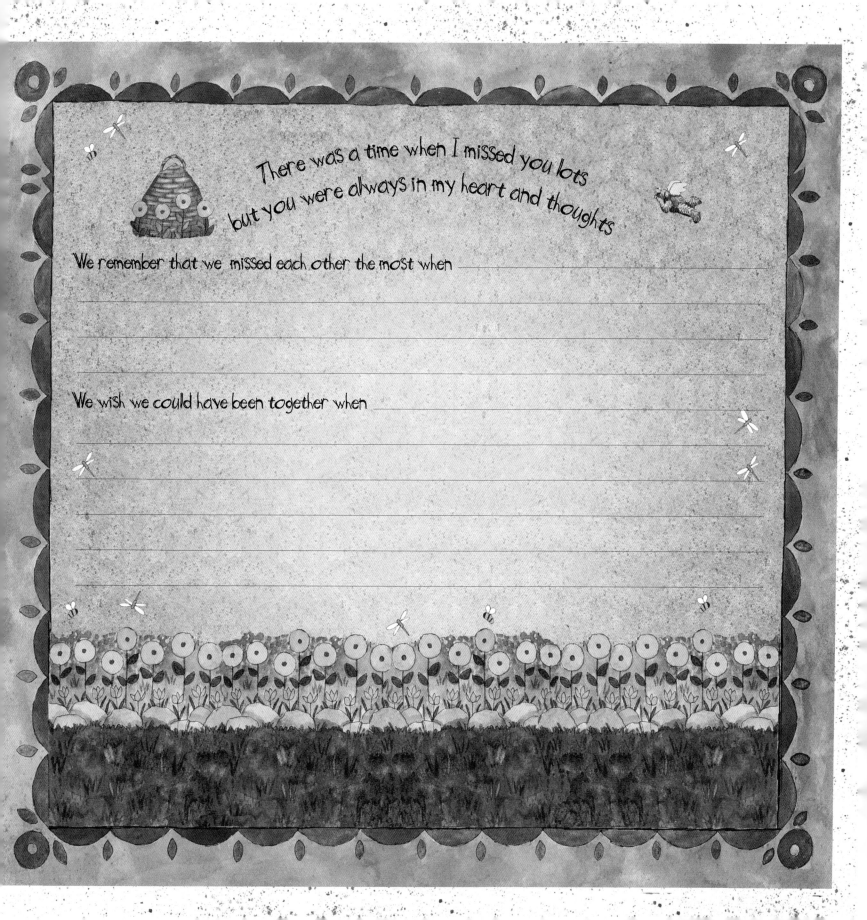

From my kitchen to yours
these are my recipes that you have adored

Recipe title _____

Ingredients   Directions

Recipe title _____

Ingredients   Directions

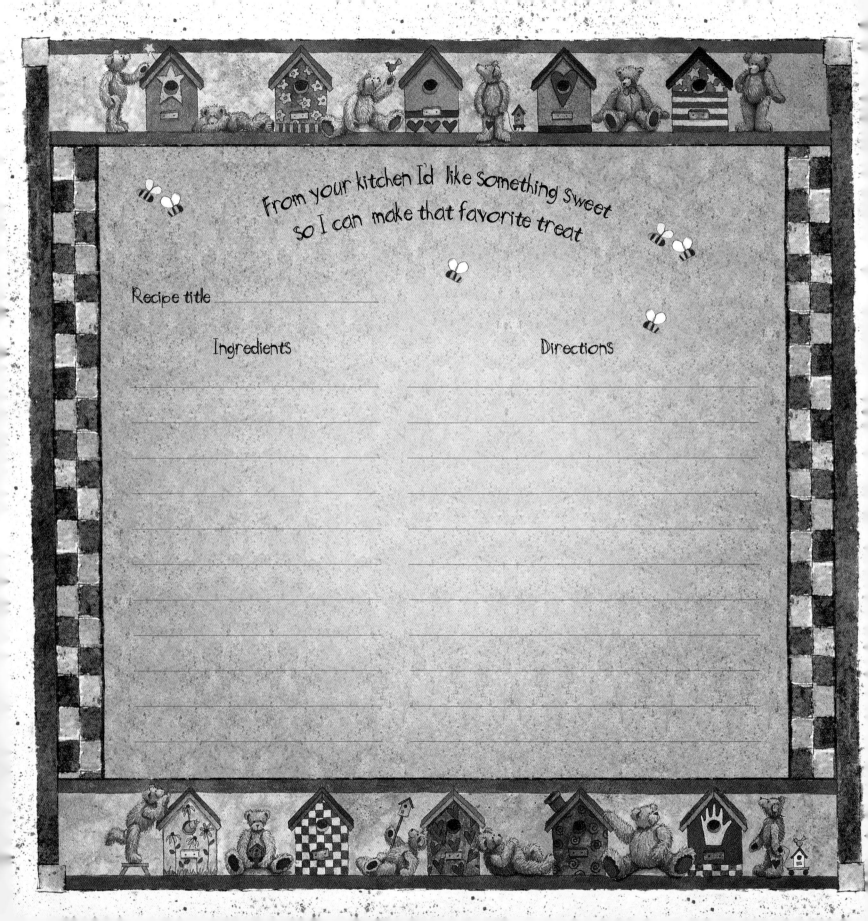

From your kitchen I'd like something sweet
so I can make that favorite treat

Recipe title _____

Ingredients   Directions

Recipe title _____

Ingredients   Directions

©T.Kogut 98

Notes of Friendship

These are a few of our favorite things
(attach pictures, clippings, and notes here)

My future wish for you
I will write down here, from me to you

I wish for you to someday _____
_____
_____
_____
_____
_____
_____
_____
_____
_____
_____
_____

Write down here your wish for me
And we will close our eyes and wait to see

I wish for you to someday _____

_____

_____

_____

_____

_____

_____

_____

_____

_____

_____

photograph

In the future, we imagine we'll be
forever friends you and me.

We imagine that we will be doing this together in five years _____

_____

_____

_____

_____

_____

_____

_____

_____

_____

_____

_____

_____

Available Record Books from Havoc

A Celebration of Memories	Heart to Heart
A Circle of Love	It's All About Me!
Baby	Memories of My Garden
Beary Special Friends	Mom
College Life	Mothers & Daughters
Couples	Mother & Son
Family	My Pregnancy
Forever Friends	Our Honeymoon
Friendship	Our Wedding
Generations	School Days
Girlfriends	Sisters
Grandmother	Tying the Knot
Grandparents	Twins
	Your First Five Years